S
MAI

SAINT MARGARET

EDITED AND PRESENTED
BY IAIN MACDONALD

FLORIS BOOKS

First published in 1993 by Floris Books

The publisher acknowledges subsidy from the
Scottish Arts Council towards the publication
of this volume.

British Library CIP Data available

ISBN 0-86315-165-5

Printed in Great Britain
by BPCC Wheatons Ltd, Exeter

Contents

Introduction

Unlike the lives of the early Celtic saints, veiled in mystery and miracle, the life of St Margaret stands clear-etched amid the complex and colourful events of her time. Written by a contemporary cleric who knew the queen well, this record of her personality and deeds gives a touching and fascinating insight into the remarkable figure of this much-loved queen.

St Margaret, an English princess, was born in Hungary about the year 1047. To understand how her parents came to be in Hungary we must go back in English history to the time of her great-grandfather, Ethelred the Unready. In 1013 Ethelred lost England to the Danish king, Sweyn (Svegn) Forkbeard, who made himself King of England.

Ethelred's third son, Edmund (Ironside) carried on the struggle against the Danes and three years later became King of England. He ruled only for six months and died in the same year (1016) whereupon the Witan, the council of Saxon nobles, chose Sweyn's son Knut (Canute) to be King of England.

Edmund Ironside however had two sons, Edmund

and Edward, who were still infants. King Knut sent the
two princes to the King of Sweden in order to have these
two claimants to the throne well out of the way. In turn
the King of Sweden sent them on to the King of
Hungary at whose court they grew up. Of Edmund we
hear no more, but Edward (called both Edward the Exile
and Edward Aetheling) married Agatha, the daughter
of Stephen, King of Hungary. Edward and Agatha
had three children, Edgar (Aetheling), Margaret and
Christina.

King Knut died in 1035 and the throne passed in
succession to his two sons, Harold I and Hardeknut. In
1042 King Hardeknut died and the Witan met to elect
the new king. Their choice fell not upon Edward, exiled
in Hungary, but upon the Ironside's younger brother
Edward (the Confessor), and this Edward was crowned
King of England and ruled until the fatal year 1066.

In 1054 Edward the Confessor sent to Hungary to
invite his nephew, Edward the Exile, to his court. Three
years later Edward the Exile returned to England with
his whole family to live at the court of King Edward.
Thus Margaret would have been about seven years old
when she came to the English court where she grew up.

Shortly after his arrival in England, Margaret's
father Edward died. Edward the Confessor had no sons
and so now Margaret's brother Edgar (Aetheling) was

next in succession to the English throne. Indeed Edward the Confessor designated him as his successor. Nevertheless on the death of Edward in 1066 the crown went to his brother-in-law Harold. This succession was hotly disputed and as is well known Harold lost his life and his kingdom at the Battle of Hastings at the hands of William (the Conqueror), Duke of Normandy. Immediately after the battle the two archbishops of England and the northern Earls chose Edgar to be King. They were however defeated and Edgar was forced to submit to the Conqueror who treated him well and took him and his family to Normandy. Two years later however Edgar and his family once more joined the northern Earls in rebellion against William, and again they were defeated. Edgar, his mother and two sisters, Margaret and Christina, escaped and sought refuge in Scotland at the court of Malcolm (III) Canmore. In the following year, 1069, she married Malcolm and became Queen of Scotland.

It is important now to follow the strands of Scottish history up to the time of this marriage which was to be of such significance for the further history of that country and of the Celtic Church.

In the year 1034, about the time when Malcolm Canmore was born (for the date of his birth is not

*certain), Malcolm's father Duncan became King of
Scotland. Duncan ruled Scotland for six years until he
was slain by his cousin Macbeth in 1040, who then
took the throne.*

*Duncan's wife was Sybil, a cousin of Siward, Earl
of Northumberland, and their eldest son was Malcolm.
Sybil fled from Macbeth taking her children with her
and sought refuge with Earl Siward. At some time
young Malcolm lived at the court of Edward the
Confessor, but he must have returned north before
Margaret and her family came to the English court, for
in 1057 with Siward's help he defeated Macbeth and
became King of Scotland. He was already a widower
with three sons when he married Margaret twelve years
later.*

*The reign of Queen Margaret and King Malcolm
Canmore is one of those significant periods of history
when new directions and currents sweep aside the old.
Enormous changes were occurring not only in Scotland,
but moreover in all of Great Britain and throughout
the Christian Church.*

*Hitherto in Scotland the leading culture had been
Gaelic-Pictish. The royal court was Gaelic-speaking.
Malcolm himself spoke Gaelic, Saxon and Latin and
as the court of Edward the Confessor was to a great*

extent also Norman he may well have understood Norman speech. Margaret herself spoke no Gaelic and in dealing with the Celtic ecclesiastics she had to use an interpreter. Through her influence and the King's Saxon sympathies (he was half English himself) the language of the court became Saxon. Saxon ways and modes now set the tone.

Already before the Conquest there were strong Norman influences in England and many Normans held lands under the Confessor. Enterprising Normans found their way north of the border and took service with Malcolm Canmore. Several Norman families made their homes in Scotland.

But most significant of all was the eclipse of the Celtic Church. Margaret and Malcolm were married by the last Celtic Bishop of St Andrews, Fothad. It was as if here the Celtic Church had given its blessing to what was to come with the new queen, for Margaret was the standard-bearer and leader of the advance of the Church of Rome oversweeping the Celtic Church. She it was who presided over the councils of churchmen and by her piety, clear reasoning, knowledge of the Scriptures and single-mindedness obtained the widespread practice of the customs and usages of the Roman Church in Scotland.

With the Celtic Church we feel the nearness, the

*immediacy of the spiritual world of divine beings
perceived directly by the Celtic saints. We feel their magic
power over wind and wave, where the force of their
saintliness made the impossible possible, the miraculous
a matter of fact, where physical reality merged indistin-
guishably into a supersensible world manifesting knowledge and even intimacy with the divine.*

*By contrast with Margaret comes that piety and
saintliness that springs from discipline and order in the
physical world. Fasts and vigils are strictly kept according to rule. Important becomes the regulation of canon
law, establishing the conventions of church observance,
from the dates of the church calendar — based on Easter
and the moveable feasts — to the details of sacramental
practice. We find, too, the growing relationship of civil
and ecclesiastical law. Vanishing slowly away is the
ancient magic and mystery, while on the fresh incoming
tide is the majesty of imperial Rome: the One Holy
Catholic and Apostolic Church, asserting a supremacy
and authority long written into the Nicene creed.*

*The emerging consciousness of the age demanded
great changes as a new social order arose: the Chris-
tianization of the last fringes of Europe signalled the
end of what we have come to call the Dark Ages, and
announced the first steps towards coherent social norms,
the rule of law and order, rights and privileges, duties*

and dependencies. In the dawning of the Middle Ages, it is the truly historical achievement of St Margaret that she was able to influence these events so effectively, with justice and holiness, and with such intelligence and purity of purpose.

By his first marriage Malcolm Canmore had three sons, two of whom became Kings of Scotland after his death. Malcolm and Margaret had eight children, three of whom also became Kings of Scotland, but here we are concerned only with the seventh child, a daughter called Matilda.

Queen Margaret's sister Christina, some time after the family had come to the court of King Malcolm, took the veil. Eventually she became Abbess of the Priory of Romsey. To this priory was sent Matilda, and against her own inclination was brought up to be a nun. From this constraint she was released in the year 1100 when Henry, William the Conqueror's son, became King of England and was looking for a wife. He married Matilda and she became Queen of England in that year. To Turgot, who had been Margaret's confessor and spiritual adviser, she gave the commission of writing the Life of her mother.

Turgot, despite his name which has a distinctly Norman ring to it, was of good Saxon family, born in

Lincolnshire, probably during the reign of King Knut. He must have taken part in the resistance against the Normans after the conquest for he escaped to Norway. Later he returned to England, and in 1074 he became a monk. Thirteen years later we find him a prior at Durham and spiritual advisor to Queen Margaret.

In 1109, during the reign of Alexander I, Fothad, the last Celtic Bishop of St Andrew's died, and Turgot was appointed as the first Roman Bishop of St Andrews.

Turgot wrote his Life of Saint Margaret in Latin. The English translation is by Forbes-Leith, published in 1884. The present text is from Metcalfe's Ancient Lives of the Scottish Saints, published in 1895.

The Life of St Margaret, Queen of Scotland

Prologue

To the honourable and excellent Matilda, Queen of the English, Turgot, a servant of the servants of St Cuthbert, sends the blessing of peace and health in this present life, and in the life which is to come the blessing of all good things.

Forasmuch as you have requested, you have also commanded me, to present to you in writing the story of the life of your mother, whose memory is held in reverence, and whose life, which was well pleasing to God, you have heard praised by so many. You have often said that in this matter my testimony is especially trustworthy, since on account of her frequent and familiar conversations with me I am acquainted with the most part of her secrets.

These your commands and desires I willingly obey; and I congratulate you, that, having been appointed Queen of the English by Him who is King of the Angels, you desire not only to hear about the life of the Queen, your mother, who ever longed for the angelic kingdom, but also to have her life constantly before you in writing so that, although you were only slightly acquainted with her face, you may at least obtain a more perfect knowledge of her virtues.

My own wish is to fulfil your commands, but I am wanting, I must confess, in the ability; the subject of this undertaking being much greater than I am able either by speech or writing to set forth.

Thus I am in a difficult strait and am drawn hither and thither. On account of the greatness of the undertaking I fear to obey; and on account of your authority and the memory of the Queen herself, of whom I am to speak, I dare not refuse. But, though I am unable to treat so great a subject in the manner it deserves, I am nevertheless bound to make it known as best I may. I owe this to the love I have for her and to the obedience which is due to your command. The grace of the Holy Spirit, which gave such efficacy to her virtues, will assist me, I trust, to narrate them.

In the first place, therefore, I desire that you, and through you others, should know that if I were to relate all that could be told respecting her, I should be thought to be flattering you under cover of your mother's praises on account of your

queenly dignity. But far be it from my grey hairs
to mingle the crime of falsehood with the virtues
of such a woman. In setting forth such virtues, I
profess, God is my Witness and Judge, that I add
nothing to the truth; but I suppress many things
lest they should seem incredible, and lest I should
be said, as the orator has it, to be decking out a
crow with the colours of a swan.

Chapter 1

Her noble descent and virtues as a Queen and as a Mother.

Many, as we read, have derived their names from a quality of the mind, so that a correspondence is revealed between the sense of their name and the grace they have received. Thus Peter was so named from "the Rock," that is Christ, on account of the firmness of his faith; and similarly John, that is "the grace of God," because of his contemplation of the Divinity and his privileged enjoyment of the Divine love; and the sons of Zebedee were called Boanerges, "the Sons of Thunder," because they thundered forth the preaching of the Gospel.

The same was true of this virtuous woman, in whom the fairness indicated by her name was surpassed by the exceeding beauty of her soul. She was called Margaret, that is, "a Pearl," and in the sight of God she was esteemed a lovely pearl by reason of her faith and good works. She was a pearl indeed to you, to me, to us all, even to Christ;

and because she was Christ's, she is all the more
ours, now that she has left us and is taken to the
Lord. This pearl I say was taken from this earth
and now shines in her place among the jewels of
the Eternal King. This I think no one will doubt,
when they have read the following account of her
life and death.

When I recall the conversations that I had with
her, seasoned as they were with the salt of wisdom,
when I think of the tears wrung from her by the
compunction of her heart, when I consider the
sobriety and steadiness of her manners and remember her affability and prudence, I rejoice
while I lament, and while lamenting I rejoice. I
rejoice, because she has passed away to God after
whom she longed; I lament, because I am not
rejoicing with her in the heavenly places. I rejoice
for her because she now sees in the land of the
living the goodness of the Lord in whom she
believed; but for myself I mourn, because as long
as I suffer the miseries of this mortal life in the
land of the dead, I am daily compelled to cry: "O
wretched man that I am, who shall deliver me
from the body of this death?"

Since, then, I am to speak of that nobility of
mind which she had in Christ, it is fitting that

something should be said first of that nobility of
birth which also distinguished her in worldly eyes.
Her grandfather was King Edmund, who, being
strong in battle and invincible by his enemies,
derived his distinctive name from the degree of
his valour, for he was called in English Ironsides.
His brother on his father's side, but not on his
mother's, was the most religious and meek Edward, who proved himself the Father of his Country; and as another Solomon, that is, a lover of
peace, protected his kingdom by peace rather
than by arms. He had a mind that subdued anger,
despised avarice, and was entirely free from pride.
And no wonder; for as he derived the glory of his
kingly rank from his ancestors, so also he derived
from them, as by hereditary right, the nobility of
his life; being descended from Edgar, King of the
English, and from Richard, Count of the Normans, his grandfathers on either side, men who
were not only most illustrious, but also most
religious. Of Edgar, in order to describe how great
he was in this world and what he was in Christ,
it may be briefly said that he was marked out
beforehand both as a King and as a lover of justice
and peace. For at his birth St Dunstan heard the
holy angels rejoicing in heaven and singing with

great joy: "Let there be peace, let there be joy in the English Church as long as this newborn boy shall hold the kingdom and Dunstan runs the course of this mortal life."

Richard, also, the father of Emma, the mother of this Edward, was an illustrious ancestor worthy of so noble a grandchild. He was a man of the greatest energy, deserving of every praise. None of his forefathers ruled the earldom of Normandy with greater prosperity and honour, or were more fervent in their love of religion. Endowed with great riches, like a second David, he was poor in spirit; exalted to be lord over his people, he was a humble servant of the servants of Christ. Among other things which he did as memorials of his love of religion, this devout worshipper of Christ built the noble monastery of Fécamp, in which he would often reside with the monks, and where, in the habit of a secular but at heart a monk, he used to serve the food of the brethren when they were eating their silent meal, and pour their drink; so that, according to the Scripture: The greater he was the more he humbled himself in all things. If any one wishes to know more fully his works of magnificence and virtue, let them read the *Acts of the Normans,* which contains his history. From

ancestors so renowned and illustrious, Edward,
their grandchild, did in no way degenerate. On
the father's side only, as was said before, he was
the brother of King Edmund, from whose son
came Margaret, who by the splendour of her
merits completes the glory of this illustrious
family.

While Margaret was still in the flower of youth,
she began to lead a life of great strictness, to love
God above all things, to occupy herself with the
study of the Holy Scriptures and to exercise her
mind therein with joy. Keen penetration of intellect was hers to understand any matter whatever
it might be; tenacity of memory to retain many
things; and a graceful facility of language to give
expression to her thoughts.

While therefore she meditated in the law of
the Lord day and night, and, like another Mary
sitting at His feet, she delighted to hear His word,
it came about that by the desire of her friends
more than her own — rather by the appointment
of God — she was married to Malcolm, son of
Duncan, the most powerful King of the Scots. But
though compelled to do the things which are of
the world, she deemed it beneath her to set her
affections upon them; for she delighted more in

good works than in abundance of riches. With things temporal she procured for herself everlasting rewards; for in heaven where her treasure was, there she had placed her heart. And because before all things she sought the kingdom of God and His righteousness, the abundant grace of the Almighty freely added to her honours and riches.

All things which became the rule of a prudent Queen were done by her; by her advice the laws of the kingdom were administered; by her zeal the true religion was spread and the people rejoiced in the prosperity of their affairs. Nothing was more firm than her faith, more constant than her favour, more enduring than her patience, weightier than her counsel, more just than her decisions, or more pleasant than her conversation.

After she had attained this high dignity, in the place where her nuptials were celebrated she immediately had built an eternal monument of her name and devotion. For she erected there the noble church in honour of the Holy Trinity with a threefold purpose: for the redemption of the King's soul, for the good of her own, and to obtain prosperity in this life and in the life that is to come for her children. This church she adorned with many precious gifts, among which, as is well

known, were not a few vessels of solid and pure
gold for the holy service of the altar, of which I
can speak with the greater certainty, since by the
Queen's commands, I myself for a long time had
them under my charge.

She placed there also a cross of incomparable
value, having upon it an image of the Saviour
which she had covered with a vestment of purest
gold and silver studded with gems; which proves
to those who behold it even now the earnestness
of her faith. To this, too, the Church of St Andrew's
bears witness, where there is preserved to this day
a most beautiful crucifix which she erected. Such
articles, those, I mean, which belong to the celebration of the divine service, were never absent
from her chamber; it seemed, so to speak, to be a
workshop for heavenly crafts. Always there were
to be seen in it copes for the cantors, chasubles,
stoles, altar-cloths, as well as other priestly vest-
ments and church ornaments. Some were in the
course of preparation, others, already finished,
were of admirable beauty.

With these works she entrusted women of
noble birth and approved conduct who were
deemed worthy to be engaged in the Queen's
service. No men were admitted among them, save

such as she allowed to accompany her when she
sometimes paid them a visit. There was no unseemly familiarity among them with the men, nor
any pert frivolity. For the Queen united such
strictness to her sweetness and such sweetness to
her strictness that all who were in her service,
men as well as women, while fearing loved her
and while loving feared her.

In her presence no one ventured to do anything wrong, or even to utter an unseemly word.
For repressing all evil in herself, there was great
gravity in her joy and something noble in her
anger. Her mirth was never expressed in immod-
erate laughter; when angry she never gave way to
fury. Always angry with her own faults, she sometimes reproved those of others with that com-
mendable anger tempered with justice which the
Psalmist enjoined, when he says: *Be angry and
sin not.* Her whole life, regulated with the greatest discretion, was, as it were, a pattern of the
virtues. Her conversation was seasoned with the
salt of wisdom: her silence was filled with good
thoughts. Her bearing so corresponded with the
gravity of her character that she might have been
born simply to show what comeliness of life is.
But briefly, in whatever she said or did, she

showed that her mind was dwelling on things
divine.

Nor did she spend less pains upon her children
than upon herself, so that they might be brought
up with the utmost care, and especially that they
might be trained in virtue. Hence because she
knew the Scripture: *He that spareth the rod hateth
his child,* she instructed the governor of the nurs-
ery as often as the children fell into such faults as
are common to their age, to curb them with
threats and the rod. By reason of their mother's
religious care they excelled many who were of
greater age in their good behaviour. Among
themselves they were always kindly and peace-
able, and the younger everywhere paid respect to
the elder. Hence, also, during the celebration of
the Mass, when they went up after their parents
to make their offerings, the younger never in any
way presumed to precede the older, but the older
were wont to go before the younger according to
their age. She would often call them to her, and,
as far as their age would allow, instruct them
concerning Christ and the faith of Christ, and
carefully endeavour to admonish them to always
fear Him.

"O my children," she would say, "fear the Lord;

for they that fear Him shall not want anything
that is good; and if you love Him, He will give
you, my darlings, prosperity in this life and eternal
felicity with all the saints."

This was the mother's desire and admonition,
the prayer which she uttered day and night with
tears for her little ones, that they might acknow-
ledge their Maker in the faith that works through
love, and acknowledging worship Him, and wor-
shipping Him, love Him in all things and above
all things, and loving Him attain to the glory of
the heavenly kingdom.

Chapter 2

Her care for the honour of the Kingdom and discipline of the Church. Abuses corrected.

We need not wonder, then, that the Queen ruled herself and her household wisely, since she was always guided by the most wise counsel of the Holy Scriptures. What I used frequently to admire in her was that amid the distraction of lawsuits and the countless affairs of the Kingdom, she gave herself with wonderful diligence to the reading of the Word of God, concerning which she used to ask profound questions of the learned men who were sitting near her. But as among them no one had a profounder intellect, so no one had the power of clearer expression. Thus it often happened that these teachers left her much more learned than when they came.

She had a religious and earnest desire for the sacred volumes, and very often her affectionate familiarity with me urged me to exert myself to obtain them for her. Nor in these things was she anxious for her own salvation alone; she sought

also that of others. And first of all, with the help
of God, she made the King himself most attentive
to works of justice, mercy, almsgiving, and other
virtues. From her also he learned to keep the
vigils of the night in prayer: from her exhortation
and example he learned to pray with sighing from
the heart and abundance of tears. I confess I
marvelled at this great miracle of the mercy of
God when I saw such earnestness of devotion in
the King, and such sorrow in the heart of a layman
when engaged in prayer.

The King as it were feared to offend a Queen
whose life was so venerable, since he clearly
perceived that Christ was truly dwelling in her
heart; he hastened all the more quickly to obey
her wishes and prudent counsels. What she refused he refused, and what she loved, he loved for
the love of her love. Hence even the books which
she used in her devotions or for reading, the King,
though unable to read, used often to handle and
examine, and when he heard from her that one
of them was dearer to her than the others, this he
regarded with kindlier affection, and would kiss
and often fondle it. Sometimes also he would send
for the goldsmith, and instruct him to adorn the
volume with gold and precious stones, and when

finished he would carry it to the Queen as a proof
of his devotion.

The Queen, for her part, herself the noblest
gem of a royal race, increased the splendour of her
husband's royal magnificence and contributed
much glory and honour to all the nobility of the
kingdom and their retainers. For she encouraged
merchants who came by land and sea from divers
lands, to bring with them many precious kinds of
merchandise which in Scotland were before un-
known. Among these, at the instigation of the
Queen, the people bought garments of various
colours, and different kinds of personal ornaments; and from that time they went about
clothed in such new and elegant fashions that
they might passed for a new race.

She also appointed a higher class of servants for
the King, so that when he walked or rode abroad
numbers of them would accompany him in state;
and this was carried out with such discipline that
wherever they came none of them was permitted
to take anything from anyone by force; nor did
any of them dare to oppress or injure the country
people or the poor in any way. Moreover, she
increased the splendour of the royal palace, so that
not only was it brightened by the different col-

oured uniforms worn in it, but the whole house was made resplendent with gold and silver; for the vessels in which the King and nobles were served with food and drink, were either of solid gold or silver, or plated with gold or silver.

The Queen did not do all this because the honour of the world delighted her, but because she felt compelled to observe what the royal dignity required of her. For when she walked in state clad in splendid apparel as became a Queen, like another Esther, she in her heart trod all these trappings beneath her feet, and bore in mind that under the gems and gold there was nothing but dust and ashes. In a word, in the midst of her exalted dignity she always took the greatest care to preserve her lowliness of mind. It was easy for her to repress all swellings of pride arising from worldly glory, inasmuch as the fleeting nature of this frail life never escaped from her thoughts. For she always remembered the text in which the miserable condition of human life is described: *Man that is born of woman, is of few days, and full of trouble. He cometh forth like a flower, and is cut down, and fleeth also as a shadow and continueth not.*

She meditated constantly also on that passage of the Blessed Apostle James, in which he says:

What is your life? It is even a vapour that appeareth for a little time, and then vanisheth away. And because as the Scripture says, *Happy is the man that feareth alway,* this venerable Queen made it easier for herself to avoid sin, as in fear and trembling she continually kept before her mind's eye the dreadful day of Judgment. Hence she frequently entreated me not to hesitate to point out and reprove in private anything which I saw amiss in her words or actions. Because I did this less frequently and sharply than she wished, she urged the duty on me and accused me of being asleep and, as it were, negligent towards her.

"The just man," she said, "shall correct me in mercy, and shall reprove me; but let not the oil of the sinner, that is the flattery, fatten my head;" for "Better are the wounds of a friend than the deceitful kisses of an enemy." She would say this because she sought censure as helping her advancement in virtue, where another might have regarded it as a disgrace.

This religious and devout Queen, while she thus in mind and word and deed journeyed on to the heavenly country, also invited others to accompany her on the undefiled way, in order that they with her might attain true happiness. The

wicked whom she saw, she admonished to become good; the good to be better, and the better
to strive to be best.

The zeal of God's house, which is the Church,
consumed her so that, aglow with apostolic faith,
she laboured to root out those unlawful things
which had sprung up within it. For when she saw
that many things were done among the Scottish
people which were contrary to the rule of the
right faith and the custom of the universal
Church, she appointed frequent councils to be
held, in order that she might somehow, through
the gift of Christ, bring back the wandering into
the way of truth. Of these councils, the most
important was that in which she alone, with a few
of her friends, for three days combatted the de-
fenders of a perverse custom with the sword of
the Spirit, that is, the Word of God. You would
have thought that there witnessed another
Helena, who formerly overcame the Jews with
the authority of the Scriptures, so now did this
Queen vanquish those who were in error. At their
discussion the King himself was present as an
assessor and chief actor, fully prepared to say and
do whatever she might direct. And as he knew
the English language quite as well as his own, he

was in this Council a most expert and watchful
interpreter for either side.

The Queen opened the proceedings by re-
marking that all who serve one God in one faith
along with the Catholic Church ought not to
vary from that Church by new or strange usages.
She then pointed out in the first place that they
were observing the fast of Lent in a way which
was not lawful, inasmuch as they were in the habit
of beginning it not with the Holy Catholic
Church on the fourth day of the week at the
beginning of Lent, but on the Monday of the
week following.

To this they answered: "The fast which we
observe, we keep according to the authority of
the Gospel, which states that Christ fasted six
weeks."

She replied by saying: "In this matter you differ
widely from the Gospel, for we read there that
the Lord fasted forty days, which you clearly do
not do. For when during the six weeks, six Lord's
days are deducted from the fast, it is plain that
only thirty and six days remain for fasting. Plainly
therefore the fast which you keep is not the forty
days enjoined by the Gospel, but one of thirty and
six days. It remains therefore for you, if you wish

to observe an abstinence of forty days, after our
Lord's example, to begin to fast with us four days
before Quadragesima; otherwise you alone will
be acting contrary to the authority of our Lord,
and in opposition to the tradition of the entire
Holy Church."

Convinced by this clear demonstration of the
truth, they henceforth began the solemnities of
the sacred fasts at the same time as Holy Church
does everywhere.

The Queen also raised another point, and
required them to explain for what reason they
neglected to receive the Sacrament of the Body
and Blood of Christ at Easter according to the
custom of the Holy and Apostolic Church.

They answered: "The Apostle speaking of those
who celebrate the Lord's Supper says: *He that
eateth and drinketh unworthily, eateth and drinketh
judgment to himself.* And hence because we ac-
knowledge that we are sinners, we fear to ap-
proach that mystery lest we should eat and drink
judgment to ourselves."

"What!" said the Queen, "Shall all who are
sinners not taste that holy mystery? No one
therefore ought to receive it, for there is not one
who is not stained with sin; not even the infant

whose life is but one day on the earth. And if no
one ought to receive it, why did the Lord when
he proclaimed the Gospel say: *Except ye shall eat
the flesh of the Son of Man, and drink His blood, ye
shall not have life in you.* But if you would understand the passage you have adduced from the
Apostle in the same way as the Father, it is evident
that you must take quite another view of it. For
the Apostle does not say that all sinners are
unworthy to receive the sacraments of salvation,
for after saying, 'he eateth and drinketh judgment
to himself,' he adds, 'Not discerning the Body of
our Lord,' that is, not distinguishing it in faith
from bodily foods, 'he eateth and drinketh judgment to himself.' But he who without confession
and penance, and with the defilement of his sins
presumes to draw near to the sacred mysteries —
he it is, I say, who eats and drinks judgment to
himself. But we who many days previously have
made confession of our faults, are chastened with
penance and fasts, and washed from the stains of
our sins by almsgiving and tears — we on the day
of the resurrection of the Lord, approaching His
Table in the Catholic Faith, receive the Body and
Blood of the Immaculate Lamb, Jesus Christ, not
to judgment, but to the remission of sins and to

the salutary preparation of our souls for the reception of eternal blessedness."

To these arguments they could make no reply, and understanding now the practices of the Church, observed them henceforth in the reception of the mystery of salvation.

Moreover, there were some in certain parts of Scotland who were wont to celebrate Masses according to I know not what barbarous rite, contrary to the custom of the whole Church. This the Queen, fired by zeal for God, sought to destroy and abolish, so that henceforth throughout the whole of Scotland there was no one who presumed to continue any such practice. It was their custom also to neglect the reverence due to the Lord's Day, and to follow their earthly occupation on that day as on others — a practice she showed them which was forbidden both by reason and authority.

"Let us reverence the Lord's Day," she said, "because of the Lord's Resurrection, which took place upon it; let us no longer do servile works on the day on which we know that we were redeemed from the bondage of the devil. This also the Blessed Pope Gregory affirms, saying: 'On the Lord's Day we ought to abstain from earthly labour, and devote ourselves wholly to prayer, in order that if during the six days we have been negligent in anything, we may on the Lord's Day expiate it by prayers.' The same Father, Gregory, after condemning one with the greatest warmth for a certain piece of earthly work which he had done on the Lord's Day, decreed that those on whose advice he had done it should be excommunicated for two months."

Unable to contradict these arguments of the wise Queen, they henceforward at her instance observed the Lord's Days with such reverence that no one dared to carry a burden on them, nor did any man venture to compel another to do so. Next she showed how utterly abominable, and to be shunned by the faithful as death itself, was the unlawful marriage of a man with his stepmother, or with the widow of his deceased brother; both of which customs had hitherto prevailed in the country. Many other abuses also which had grown up contrary to the rule of faith and the institutions and observances of the Church, she likewise in this Council succeeded in condemning and expelling from the Kingdom. For whatever she proposed, she so supported with the testimony of the Holy Scriptures and with citations from the holy Fathers, that no one on the opposite side could say anything at all against it; nay, rather, laying aside their obstinacy and yielding to reason, they willingly undertook to adopt whatever she desired.

Chapter 3

Her charity towards the poor. Her manner of passing Lent. Her prayerfulness.

Thus the venerable Queen, who by the help of God had endeavoured to cleanse His house from defilements and errors, was found day by day as the Holy Spirit illuminated her heart, more and more meet to become His temple. And such I well know she truly was, for I both saw the works which she did outwardly, and knew her conscience, for she revealed it to me. She condescended to converse with me in the most familiar way, and to disclose to me her secret thoughts; not because there was anything good in me, but because she thought there was. When she conversed with me concerning the salvation of the soul and the sweetness of the life which is eternal, she uttered words so full of all grace that the Holy Spirit, which truly dwelt in her heart, evidently spoke by her lips. And so deeply was she moved while speaking, that it might have been thought that she would be wholly dissolved in tears, and at her compunction I also was moved to weeping.

Beyond all whom I have ever known she devoted herself to prayer and fasting, and to works of mercy and almsgiving. Let me speak first of her prayerfulness. In a church no one was ever more silent or composed, and in prayer no one was ever more earnest. For while in the house of God she would never speak of worldly matters, nor do anything which savoured of the earth. It was her custom there only to pray, in prayer to pour forth her tears. In the body only was she here on earth; her soul was with God; for besides God and the things which are God's, in her pure supplications she sought nothing. But what shall I say of her fasting? This only, that by her too great abstinence she brought upon herself a very serious infirmity.

To these two, that is, to prayer and fasting, she joined the gifts of mercy. For what could be more compassionate than her heart? What more gentle to the needy? Not only would she give her goods to the poor, but if she could, she would have freely given herself. She was poorer than any of her paupers, for they, having nothing, desired to have, but she was anxious to dispose what she had. When she walked or rode out in public, crowds

of poor people, orphans and widows, flocked to
her as they would to a most beloved mother, and
none of them ever left her without being com-
forted. And when all she had brought with her
for the use of the needy had been distributed, she
used to receive from her attendants and the rich
who accompanied her their garments and anything else they had with them at the time, to
bestow upon the poor, so that no one might ever
go away from her in distress. Nor did those who
were with her take this ill; they rather strove
among themselves to offer her what they had,
since they knew for certain that she would pay
them the double of what they had given.

Now and then she took something or other,
whatever it might be, from the King's private
property to give to a poor person, and the King
always took this pious plundering in good part
and pleasantly. On Maundy Thursday and at High
Mass he used to make an offering of gold coins,
and some of these she would often piously steal
and give away to the beggar who was importun-
ing her for alms. Often indeed the King, who was
quite aware of what she was doing, though he
pretended not to know anything about it, was
greatly amused at this kind of theft, and some-

times, when he caught her in the act with the coins in her hand, would jocularly threaten to have her arrested, tried, and condemned. Nor was it to the poor of her own people alone that she exhibited the abundance of her cheerful and open-handed charity, those also were sharers of her bounty whom the fame of her liberality drew towards her from almost every other nation. Of a truth, to her may be applied the Scripture: He hath dispersed; he hath given to the poor; his righteousness endureth for ever.

Who can tell the number of English captives of all ranks carried away from their own country by the violence of war, and reduced to slavery, whom she restored to liberty by paying their ransom? She sent secret spies everywhere throughout the provinces of Scotland to ascertain who among the captives were oppressed with the cruellest bondage or were the more inhumanely treated, and to report privately to her where they were and by whom they were ill-treated; and, commiserating them from the bottom of her heart, she hastened to their assistance, paid their ransom, and restored them to freedom.

At that time there were very many throughout the kingdom of Scotland who, isolated in their

cells, were leading lives of great strictness, in the
flesh but not according to the flesh, for though
on this earth, they were living the life of angels.
In these the Queen venerated Christ and loved
Him, and frequently occupied herself in visiting
and conversing with them, and used to commend
herself to their prayers. And since she could not
prevail upon them to accept from her any earthly
gift, she used to earnestly entreat them to honour
her by prescribing for her some work of almsgiving or mercy; and forthwith this devout woman
did whatever they desired, either by rescuing the
poor out of their poverty or by relieving the
afflicted from the miseries by which they were
oppressed.

Since the Church of St Andrew was much
frequented by the devout, who flocked to it from
all sides, she erected dwellings on either shore of
the sea which divides Lothian from Scotland, that,
after the fatigues of their journey, pilgrims and the
poor might take shelter and rest, and there find
already prepared for them all they needed for the
refreshment of the body; for she had appointed
servants whose exclusive duty was always to have
in readiness everything that these wayfarers might
need, and to attend to them with the greatest care.

She also provided ships for the transport of these
pilgrims, both coming and going; nor was any toll
ever levied from those who were ferried across.

As I have spoken of the daily manner of life of
this venerable Queen, and of her daily works of
mercy, I will now attempt to give a brief account
of how she used to spend the forty days before
Christmas and the whole season of Lent. After she
had rested a little at the beginning of the night,
she went into the church, and there alone she
completed first the Matins of the Holy Trinity,
next the Matins of the Holy Cross, and then the
Matins of Our Lady. When these were ended she
began the Offices of the Dead, and after these the
Psalter, nor did she cease until she had gone
through it. While the priests were saying the
Matins and Lauds at the fitting hour, she either
finished the Psalter she had begun, or if she had
finished it, began it a second time. When she had
gone through the office of the Matins and Lauds,
she returned to her chamber, and along with the
King himself washed the feet of six poor persons,
and used to give them something wherewith they
might relieve their poverty. It was the Chamber-
lain's especial duty to bring these poor people in
every night before the Queen's arrival, so that she

might find them ready when she came to wait upon them. After she had waited upon them, she betook herself to rest and sleep.

When the day dawned she rose from bed, and continued for a long time in prayer and reading the Psalms, and whilst reading them performed this work of mercy — nine little orphan children, who were utterly destitute, she had brought in to her at the first hour of the day so that she might feed them. She ordered soft food, such as little children delight in, to be prepared for them daily; and when the little ones were brought to her, she did not think it beneath her to take them on her knee and make little sups for them and feed them herself with the spoons of her own table.

Thus the Queen, honoured by all the people, performed for Christ's sake the office of a most devoted servant and mother. To her the words of the Blessed Job might very fittingly be applied: *From my infancy mercy grew up with me, and it came out with me from my mother's womb.*

While this was going on, it was the custom to bring three hundred poor people into the royal hall, and when they had been seated round it in order, the King and Queen came in, and the doors were shut by the servants, for with the exception of the chaplains, certain religious, and a few attendants, no one was permitted to witness their almsgivings. The King on the one side, and the Queen on the other, waited upon Christ in the person of His poor, and with great devotion served them with food and drink, which had been specially prepared for this purpose. When this was finished, the Queen used to go into the Church and there offer herself a sacrifice to God with many prayers, sighs, and tears. For besides the Hours of the Holy Trinity, the Holy Cross, and the Holy Mary, recited within the space of a day and a night, she would on these holy days repeat the Psalter twice or thrice, and before the celebration of the public Mass cause five or six Masses to be sung privately in her presence.

By the time these things were finished, the time for eating was at hand, but before taking her own food she fed twenty-four poor people, whom she humbly waited upon herself. For besides the many alms-deeds I have spoken of already, she supported poor people to this number, that is, twenty-four, throughout the whole course of the year as long as she lived. These she desired to live near to wherever she herself was living, and to

accompany her wherever she went. After she had
devoutly waited upon Christ in these, she used to
refresh her own feeble body. In this meal, since
according to the Apostle we ought not to make
provision for the lust of the flesh, she hardly
allowed herself the necessaries of life, for she ate
only to sustain life and not to please her palate.
Her light and frugal meal excited rather than
satisfied her hunger. She seemed to taste her food,
not to take it.

From this let it be considered, I beseech you,
how great her abstinence was when she fasted,
when such was her abstinence when she feasted.
And though her whole life was one of great
temperance, yet during these fasts, that is, during
the forty days preceding Easter and Christmas,
the abstinence with which she was in the habit
of afflicting herself was incredible. Hence, on
account of her excessive fasting, she suffered up
to the end of her life from a very acute pain in
the stomach. Nevertheless, her bodily infirmity
did not impair her virtue in good works. Assidu-
ous in reading the sacred Scriptures, instant in
prayer, and unceasing in almsgiving, she exercised
herself continually and watchfully in all things
pertaining to God. And because she knew the

Scripture: *Whom the Lord loveth, he chasteneth, and scourgeth every son whom he receiveth,* she accepted the pains of her body willingly, and with patience and thanksgiving, as the stripes of a most gracious Father.

Since therefore she was devoted to these and similar works, and struggled with her continual infirmities, God's strength — to use the words of the Apostle — was made perfect in her weakness; and going on from strength to strength, she was each day made better. Forsaking in her heart all earthly things, she longed with her whole soul for the things of heaven, even thirsted for them, crying out with her heart and voice with the Psalmist: *My soul thirsteth for God, for the living God; when shall I come and appear before God?*

Let others admire the tokens of miracles which they see in others, I, for my part, admire much more the works of mercy which I saw in Margaret. Miracles are common to the evil and to the good, but the works of true piety and charity belong to the good alone. The former sometimes indicate holiness, but the latter are holiness itself. Let us, I say, admire in Margaret the things which made her a saint, rather than the miracles, if she did any, which might only have indicated that she

was one to men. Let us more worthily admire her
as one in whom, because of her devotion to
justice, piety, mercy, and love, we see rather the
works of the ancient Fathers than their miracles.
Nevertheless, it will not be out of place if I here
narrate one incident which seems to me to indicate the holiness of her life.

She had a book of the Gospels beautifully
adorned with jewels and gold, and ornamented
with the figures of the four Evangelists, painted
and gilt. The capital letters throughout the volume were also resplendent with gold. For this
volume she had always a greater affection than
she had for any others she was in the habit of
reading. It happened that while the person who
was carrying it was crossing a ford, he let the
volume, which had been carelessly folded in a
wrapper, fall into the middle of the stream, and,
ignorant of what had occurred, he quietly continued his journey. But when he afterwards
wished to produce the book, he, for the first time,
became aware that he had lost it. It was sought
for a long time, but was not found. At length it
was found at the bottom of the river, lying open,
so that its leaves were kept in constant motion by
the action of the water, and the little coverings of

silk which protected the letters of gold from being injured by the contact of the leaves, were carried away by the force of the current.

Who would imagine that the book would be worth anything after what had happened to it? Who would believe that even a single letter would have been visible in it? Yet of a truth it was taken up out of the middle of the river so perfect, uninjured, and free from damage, that it looked as though it had not even been touched by the water. For the whiteness of the leaves, and the form of the letters throughout the whole of the volume remained exactly as they were before it fell into the river, except that on the margin of the leaves, towards the edge, some trace of the water could with difficulty be detected. The book was conveyed to the Queen, and the miracle reported to her at the same time, and she having given thanks to Christ, esteemed the volume much more highly than she did before. Wherefore let others consider what they should think of this, but as for me I am of opinion that this miracle was wrought by our Lord because of His love for this venerable Queen.

Chapter 4

The Queen's preparations for her end. Her sickness and happy death.

Meantime, while Almighty God was preparing everlasting rewards for her works of devotion, she was preparing herself, with more than her usual carefulness, for entering another life. For, as her own word a little after showed, it would appear that her own departure from this life and certain other events were known to her long before they occurred.

Therefore summoning me to come to her privately, she began to recount to me the entire story of her life, and as she proceeded shed floods of tears. In short, so great was her compunction while she conversed with me, and out of her compunction there sprang such an abundance of tears, that, as it seemed to me, there was, beyond all doubt, nothing which she might not at that time have obtained from Christ. As she wept I also wept; thus for a time we wept and at times were silent, since we were unable to give utterance to our words. The flame, as it were, of the compunction which consumed her heart reached my own soul also, borne into it by the spiritual fervour of her words. And when I heard the words of the Holy Ghost speaking by her tongue and clearly perceived her conscience revealed by her words, I judged myself unworthy of the grace of so great a familiarity.

When she had ceased to speak of the things which it was needful for her to speak, she began to address me again, saying: "Farewell, I shall not remain long with you in this life; but you will survive me for a considerable time. Two things, therefore, I beg of you. One is, that as long as you live you will remember me in your prayers and at the Mass; the other is, that you will take some care of my sons and daughters, pour out your affection upon them, above all things teach them to fear and love God, and never cease from instructing them; and when you see any of them exalted to the height of earthly dignity, then at once, as a father or a teacher in the highest sense, go to him, warn, and when circumstances require it, censure him, lest, on account of a passing honour, he be puffed up with pride, or offend God with avarice, or through the prosperity of the world neglect

the blessedness of life eternal. These are the
things," she said, "which I ask you, as in the sight
of God who is now present along with us two, to
promise me that you will carefully do."

At these words I again burst into tears and
promised her that I would carefully perform what
she had asked me; for I did not dare to oppose
one whom I heard unhesitatingly predict what
was to come to pass. The truth of her prediction
has now been verified by the things which now
are; since I live and she is dead and I see her off-
spring raised to dignity and honour. Thus having
finished her conference with me and being about
to return home I said farewell to the Queen for
the last time; for I saw her face no more.

Not long after this she was attacked by an
illness more severe than usual, and was purified
by the fire of a tedious sickness before the day on
which she was called away. I will describe her
death as I heard it narrated by her priest, whom,
on account of his simplicity, innocence, and purity, she loved more intimately than the others,
and who after her death gave himself to Christ in
perpetual service for her soul, and having put on
the monk's habit, offered himself as a sacrifice for
her at the tomb of the incorrupt body of the most

holy Father Cuthbert. Towards the end of the Queen's life he was continually with her, and with his prayers commended her soul to Christ as it was leaving the body. Of her decease as he saw it he more than once gave me a full account, for I often asked him, and he used to do so with tears in his eyes.

"For a little more than half a year," he said, "she was unable to sit on horseback, and could seldom rise from her bed. On the fourth day before her death, while the King was absent on an expedition, and at so great a distance that it was impossible for any messenger, however swift he might be, to bring her tidings of what was happening to him that day, she became sadder than usual, and said to me as I sat beside her: 'Perhaps so great a calamity is today befalling the realm of Scotland as has not overtaken it for many ages.'

"When I heard the words I did not pay much attention to them; but a few days later a messenger came who informed us that the King had been slain on the very day the Queen had spoken about him. As if foreseeing the future, she had urged him not to go with the army, but it chanced, I know not from what cause, that he did not follow her advice.

"When the fourth day after the King's death approached, her weakness having abated a little, she went into her oratory to hear Mass, and there she took care to fortify herself beforehand for her departure, which was already at hand, with the holy Viaticum of the Body and Blood of the Lord. Refreshed with this health-giving food, she went back to bed, for her former pains returned with greater severity. Towards the end her suffering increased and she was very sorely troubled. What can I do? Why do I delay? As if I were able to defer the death of my Queen, or lengthen her life — thus I fear to come to the end. But: *All flesh is grass, and all the glory thereof as the flower of the grass; the grass withereth and the flower falleth.*

"Her face had already grown pale with death when she directed that I and other ministers of the sacred Altar with me should stand beside her and commend her soul to Christ with our psalms. Moreover, she requested that a cross should be brought to her, called the Black Cross, which she had always held in the greatest veneration. But as the chest in which it was kept could not be quickly opened, the Queen said with a deep sigh: 'O unhappy that we are! O guilty that we are!

Shall we not be permitted one last look of the
Holy Cross!'

"When at length it was taken out of the chest
and brought to her, she received it with reverence,
and frequently tried to embrace it and kiss it, and
to sign her eyes and face with it. Every part of her
body was already growing cold, yet as long as the
warmth of life throbbed in her breast she continued in prayer. She repeated the whole of the
Fiftieth Psalm, and while so doing, placed the
Cross before her eyes and held it there with both
her hands.

"It was whilst she was doing this that her son,
who now holds in this kingdom the helm of the
State, arrived from the army and entered the
Queen's chamber. What must then have been his
distress? What his agony of soul? He stood there
in a strait, with everything against him; whither
to turn he knew not. He had come to announce
to his mother that his father and brother had been
slain, and he found his mother, whom he loved
most dearly, at the point of death. Whom to
lament first he knew not. Yet the loss of his dearest
mother, whom he saw lying almost dead before
his eyes, pierced his heart with the sharpest pain.
Besides all this, the condition of the kingdom was

filling him with the deepest anxiety, for he well
knew that disturbances would follow on the
death of his father. On every side he was met by
sadness and trouble. The Queen when lying, as it
seemed to those present, rapt in agony, suddenly
collected her strength and addressed her son. She
asked him what news concerning his father and
his brother. He was unwilling to tell her the truth,
fearing if she heard of their death she herself
would immediately die; and answered that they
were well. But she, sighing deeply, said: 'I know it,
my son; I know it. By this holy Cross, by the bond
of our blood, I adjure thee to tell me the truth.'

"When he was thus pressed, he told her all as
it had happened. What could she do? Who would
have believed that in the midst of so many adver-
sities she would not murmur against God? All in
one moment she had lost her husband and her
son, and a disease tormented her to the point of
death. But amidst all these things she sinned not
with her lips, nor spoke foolishly against God,
rather she raised her eyes and hands to heaven and
broke forth into praise and thanksgiving, saying:
'Praise and thanks I give to Thee, Almighty God,
that Thou hast been pleased that I should endure
such great afflictions at my departing, and art

pleased, as I trust, that, through enduring these afflictions, I should be cleansed from some stain of sin.'

"She now felt that death was close at hand, and at once began the prayer which is said by the priest after he receives the Body and Blood of our Lord, saying: 'Lord Jesus Christ, who, according to the will of the Father, through the co-operation of the Holy Ghost, hast by Thy death given life to the world, deliver me.'

"As she was saying the words 'Deliver me,' her soul was delivered from the chains of the body, and departed to Christ, the author of true liberty, whom she had always loved, and by whom she was made a partaker of the happiness of the saints, the example of whose virtues she had followed. With such tranquillity and such quietude was her departure, that there can be no doubt that her soul passed to the land of eternal rest and peace. It was remarkable that her face which, when she was dying, had exhibited the usual pallor of death, was afterwards suffused with red and white tints, so that it might have been believed that she was not dead but sleeping. Her corpse was honourably shrouded as became a Queen, and we bore it to the Church of the Holy Trinity, which she herself had built; and there, as she had directed, we committed it to the grave opposite the Altar and the venerable sign of the Holy Cross which she had erected. And thus her body now rests in the place where she was wont to humble herself with vigils, prayers, shedding of tears, and prostrations."